Made in the USA
Columbia, SC
24 November 2020

Date: ____________________

This Morning My Mood Is:

I'm Looking Forward To the Day Because: ____________________

Three Things I'm Grateful for Today

1. ____________________
2. ____________________
3. ____________________

The Nice Things From Today

I Did for Someone

Someone Did for Me

Notes and Thoughts on the Day

Tonight My Mood Is:

Date:

This Morning My Mood Is:

I'm Looking Forward To the Day Because:

Three Things I'm Grateful for Today

1.

2.

3.

The Nice Things From Today

I Did for Someone

Someone Did for Me

Notes and Thoughts on the Day

Tonight My Mood Is:       

Date: ____________________

This Morning My Mood Is:

I'm Looking Forward To the Day Because: ____________________

Three Things I'm Grateful for Today

1. ____________________
2. ____________________
3. ____________________

The Nice Things From Today

I Did for Someone

Someone Did for Me

Notes and Thoughts on the Day

Tonight My Mood Is:

Date: ____________________

This Morning My Mood Is:

I'm Looking Forward To the Day Because: ____________________

Three Things I'm Grateful for Today

1. ____________________
2. ____________________
3. ____________________

The Nice Things From Today

I Did for Someone

Someone Did for Me

Notes and Thoughts on the Day

Tonight My Mood Is:

Date: ______________________

This Morning My Mood Is:	😆 😃 🙂 😐 🙁 😢 😫

I'm Looking Forward To the Day Because: ______________________

____

____

Three Things I'm Grateful for Today

1. ______________________
2. ______________________
3. ______________________

The Nice Things From Today

I Did for Someone	Someone Did for Me
______________________	______________________
______________________	______________________
______________________	______________________

Notes and Thoughts on the Day

____

____

____

____

____

Tonight My Mood Is:	😆 😃 🙂 😐 🙁 😢 😫

Date: ______________________

This Morning My Mood Is:

I'm Looking Forward To the Day Because: ______________________

Three Things I'm Grateful for Today

1. ______________________

2. ______________________

3. ______________________

The Nice Things From Today

I Did for Someone

Someone Did for Me

Notes and Thoughts on the Day

Tonight My Mood Is:      

Date: ______________________

This Morning My Mood Is:

I'm Looking Forward To the Day Because: ______________________

Three Things I'm Grateful for Today

1. ______________________
2. ______________________
3. ______________________

The Nice Things From Today

I Did for Someone

Someone Did for Me

Notes and Thoughts on the Day

Tonight My Mood Is:

Date: ____________________

This Morning My Mood Is:

I'm Looking Forward To the Day Because: ____________________

Three Things I'm Grateful for Today

1. ____________________
2. ____________________
3. ____________________

The Nice Things From Today

I Did for Someone

Someone Did for Me

Notes and Thoughts on the Day

Tonight My Mood Is:       

Date: ____________________

This Morning My Mood Is:

I'm Looking Forward To the Day Because: ____________________

Three Things I'm Grateful for Today

1. ____________________
2. ____________________
3. ____________________

The Nice Things From Today

I Did for Someone

Someone Did for Me

Notes and Thoughts on the Day

Tonight My Mood Is:

Date:

This Morning My Mood Is:

I'm Looking Forward To the Day Because:

Three Things I'm Grateful for Today

1.

2.

3.

The Nice Things From Today

I Did for Someone

Someone Did for Me

Notes and Thoughts on the Day

Tonight My Mood Is:       

Date: ____________________

This Morning My Mood Is:

I'm Looking Forward To the Day Because: ____________________

Three Things I'm Grateful for Today

1. ____________________
2. ____________________
3. ____________________

The Nice Things From Today

I Did for Someone	Someone Did for Me

Notes and Thoughts on the Day

Tonight My Mood Is:

Date: ______________________

This Morning My Mood Is:	😄 😃 🙂 😐 ☹️ 😟 😠

I'm Looking Forward To the Day Because: ______________________

____

____

Three Things I'm Grateful for Today
1. ______________________
2. ______________________
3. ______________________

The Nice Things From Today

I Did for Someone	Someone Did for Me
______________________	______________________
______________________	______________________
______________________	______________________

Notes and Thoughts on the Day

____

____

____

____

____

Tonight My Mood Is:	😄 😃 🙂 😐 ☹️ 😟 😠

Date: ______________________

This Morning My Mood Is:

I'm Looking Forward To the Day Because: ______________________

Three Things I'm Grateful for Today

1. ______________________
2. ______________________
3. ______________________

The Nice Things From Today

I Did for Someone	Someone Did for Me

Notes and Thoughts on the Day

Tonight My Mood Is:

Date:

This Morning My Mood Is:

I'm Looking Forward To the Day Because:

Three Things I'm Grateful for Today

1.

2.

3.

The Nice Things From Today

I Did for Someone

Someone Did for Me

Notes and Thoughts on the Day

Tonight My Mood Is:       

Date: ____________________

This Morning My Mood Is:

I'm Looking Forward To the Day Because: ____________________

Three Things I'm Grateful for Today

1. ____________________

2. ____________________

3. ____________________

The Nice Things From Today

I Did for Someone	Someone Did for Me

Notes and Thoughts on the Day

Tonight My Mood Is:

Date: ____________________

This Morning My Mood Is:	😄 😃 🙂 😐 ☹️ 😢 😠

I'm Looking Forward To the Day Because: ____________________

____

____

Three Things I'm Grateful for Today

1. ____________________
2. ____________________
3. ____________________

The Nice Things From Today

I Did for Someone	Someone Did for Me

Notes and Thoughts on the Day

____

____

____

____

____

Tonight My Mood Is:	😄 😃 🙂 😐 ☹️ 😢 😠

Date: ____________________

This Morning My Mood Is:

I'm Looking Forward To the Day Because: ____________________

Three Things I'm Grateful for Today

1. ____________________
2. ____________________
3. ____________________

The Nice Things From Today

I Did for Someone

Someone Did for Me

Notes and Thoughts on the Day

Tonight My Mood Is:

Date: ____________________

This Morning My Mood Is:

I'm Looking Forward To the Day Because: ____________________

Three Things I'm Grateful for Today

1. ____________________

2. ____________________

3. ____________________

The Nice Things From Today

I Did for Someone

Someone Did for Me

Notes and Thoughts on the Day

Tonight My Mood Is:

Date: ____________________

This Morning My Mood Is:

I'm Looking Forward To the Day Because: ____________________

Three Things I'm Grateful for Today

1. ____________________

2. ____________________

3. ____________________

The Nice Things From Today

I Did for Someone

Someone Did for Me

Notes and Thoughts on the Day

Tonight My Mood Is:

Date:

This Morning My Mood Is:

I'm Looking Forward To the Day Because:

Three Things I'm Grateful for Today

1.
2.
3.

The Nice Things From Today

I Did for Someone

Someone Did for Me

Notes and Thoughts on the Day

Tonight My Mood Is:

Date: ____________________

This Morning My Mood Is:

I'm Looking Forward To the Day Because: ____________________

Three Things I'm Grateful for Today

1. ____________________
2. ____________________
3. ____________________

The Nice Things From Today

I Did for Someone

Someone Did for Me

Notes and Thoughts on the Day

Tonight My Mood Is:

Date:

This Morning My Mood Is:

I'm Looking Forward To the Day Because:

Three Things I'm Grateful for Today

1.

2.

3.

The Nice Things From Today

I Did for Someone

Someone Did for Me

Notes and Thoughts on the Day

Tonight My Mood Is:

Date: ____________________

This Morning My Mood Is:

I'm Looking Forward To the Day Because: ____________________

Three Things I'm Grateful for Today

1. ____________________

2. ____________________

3. ____________________

The Nice Things From Today

I Did for Someone

Someone Did for Me

Notes and Thoughts on the Day

Tonight My Mood Is:

Date: ____________________

This Morning My Mood Is:

I'm Looking Forward To the Day Because: ____________________

Three Things I'm Grateful for Today

1. ____________________
2. ____________________
3. ____________________

The Nice Things From Today

I Did for Someone	Someone Did for Me

Notes and Thoughts on the Day

Tonight My Mood Is:

Date:

This Morning My Mood Is:

I'm Looking Forward To the Day Because:

Three Things I'm Grateful for Today

1.

2.

3.

The Nice Things From Today

I Did for Someone

Someone Did for Me

Notes and Thoughts on the Day

Tonight My Mood Is:

Date: ______________________

This Morning My Mood Is: 😄 😀 🙂 😐 ☹️ 😟 😠

I'm Looking Forward To the Day Because: ______________________

Three Things I'm Grateful for Today

1. ______________________
2. ______________________
3. ______________________

The Nice Things From Today

I Did for Someone	Someone Did for Me

Notes and Thoughts on the Day

Tonight My Mood Is: 😄 😀 🙂 😐 ☹️ 😟 😠

Date: ____________________

This Morning My Mood Is:

I'm Looking Forward To the Day Because: ____________________

Three Things I'm Grateful for Today

1. ____________________
2. ____________________
3. ____________________

The Nice Things From Today

I Did for Someone

Someone Did for Me

Notes and Thoughts on the Day

Tonight My Mood Is:

Date:

This Morning My Mood Is:

I'm Looking Forward To the Day Because:

Three Things I'm Grateful for Today

1.

2.

3.

The Nice Things From Today

I Did for Someone

Someone Did for Me

Notes and Thoughts on the Day

Tonight My Mood Is:

Date: ______________________

This Morning My Mood Is:

I'm Looking Forward To the Day Because: ______________________

Three Things I'm Grateful for Today

1. ______________________
2. ______________________
3. ______________________

The Nice Things From Today

I Did for Someone

Someone Did for Me

Notes and Thoughts on the Day

Tonight My Mood Is:

Date:

This Morning My Mood Is:

I'm Looking Forward To the Day Because:

Three Things I'm Grateful for Today

1.

2.

3.

The Nice Things From Today

I Did for Someone

Someone Did for Me

Notes and Thoughts on the Day

Tonight My Mood Is:

Date: ____________________

This Morning My Mood Is:

I'm Looking Forward To the Day Because: ____________________

Three Things I'm Grateful for Today

1. ____________________
2. ____________________
3. ____________________

The Nice Things From Today

I Did for Someone

Someone Did for Me

Notes and Thoughts on the Day

Tonight My Mood Is:

Date:

This Morning My Mood Is:

I'm Looking Forward To the Day Because:

Three Things I'm Grateful for Today

1.

2.

3.

The Nice Things From Today

I Did for Someone

Someone Did for Me

Notes and Thoughts on the Day

Tonight My Mood Is:       

Date: ____________________

This Morning My Mood Is:

I'm Looking Forward To the Day Because: ____________________

Three Things I'm Grateful for Today

1. ____________________

2. ____________________

3. ____________________

The Nice Things From Today

I Did for Someone

Someone Did for Me

Notes and Thoughts on the Day

Tonight My Mood Is:

Date: ______________________

This Morning My Mood Is: ☐ ☐ ☐ ☐ ☐ ☐ ☐

I'm Looking Forward To the Day Because: ______________________

____

____

Three Things I'm Grateful for Today

1. ______________________
2. ______________________
3. ______________________

The Nice Things From Today

I Did for Someone	Someone Did for Me

Notes and Thoughts on the Day

____

____

____

____

____

Tonight My Mood Is: ☐ ☐ ☐ ☐ ☐ ☐ ☐

Date: ______________________

This Morning My Mood Is:

I'm Looking Forward To the Day Because: ______________________

Three Things I'm Grateful for Today

1. ______________________
2. ______________________
3. ______________________

The Nice Things From Today

I Did for Someone	Someone Did for Me

Notes and Thoughts on the Day

Tonight My Mood Is:

Date: ____________________

This Morning My Mood Is:

I'm Looking Forward To the Day Because: ____________________

Three Things I'm Grateful for Today

1. ____________________
2. ____________________
3. ____________________

The Nice Things From Today

I Did for Someone

Someone Did for Me

Notes and Thoughts on the Day

Tonight My Mood Is:

Date: ____________________

This Morning My Mood Is:

I'm Looking Forward To the Day Because: ____________________

Three Things I'm Grateful for Today

1. ____________________
2. ____________________
3. ____________________

The Nice Things From Today

I Did for Someone	Someone Did for Me

Notes and Thoughts on the Day

Tonight My Mood Is:

Date: ____________________

This Morning My Mood Is:

I'm Looking Forward To the Day Because: ____________________

Three Things I'm Grateful for Today

1. ____________________

2. ____________________

3. ____________________

The Nice Things From Today

I Did for Someone

Someone Did for Me

Notes and Thoughts on the Day

Tonight My Mood Is:       

Date: ______________________

This Morning My Mood Is:

I'm Looking Forward To the Day Because: ______________________

Three Things I'm Grateful for Today

1. ______________________

2. ______________________

3. ______________________

The Nice Things From Today

I Did for Someone

Someone Did for Me

Notes and Thoughts on the Day

Tonight My Mood Is:

Date:

This Morning My Mood Is:

I'm Looking Forward To the Day Because:

Three Things I'm Grateful for Today

1.

2.

3.

The Nice Things From Today

I Did for Someone

Someone Did for Me

Notes and Thoughts on the Day

Tonight My Mood Is:

Date: ____________________

This Morning My Mood Is:

I'm Looking Forward To the Day Because: ____________________

Three Things I'm Grateful for Today

1. ____________________
2. ____________________
3. ____________________

The Nice Things From Today

I Did for Someone

Someone Did for Me

Notes and Thoughts on the Day

Tonight My Mood Is:

Date: ____________________

This Morning My Mood Is:

I'm Looking Forward To the Day Because: ____________________

Three Things I'm Grateful for Today

1. ____________________
2. ____________________
3. ____________________

The Nice Things From Today

I Did for Someone

Someone Did for Me

Notes and Thoughts on the Day

Tonight My Mood Is:

Date: ____________________

This Morning My Mood Is:

I'm Looking Forward To the Day Because: ____________________

Three Things I'm Grateful for Today

1. ____________________
2. ____________________
3. ____________________

The Nice Things From Today

I Did for Someone

Someone Did for Me

Notes and Thoughts on the Day

Tonight My Mood Is:

Date: ____________________

This Morning My Mood Is:

I'm Looking Forward To the Day Because: ____________________

Three Things I'm Grateful for Today

1. ____________________
2. ____________________
3. ____________________

The Nice Things From Today

I Did for Someone

Someone Did for Me

Notes and Thoughts on the Day

Tonight My Mood Is:

Date: ______________________

This Morning My Mood Is:

I'm Looking Forward To the Day Because: ______________________

Three Things I'm Grateful for Today

1. ______________________
2. ______________________
3. ______________________

The Nice Things From Today

I Did for Someone

Someone Did for Me

Notes and Thoughts on the Day

Tonight My Mood Is:       

Date: ______________________

This Morning My Mood Is:	😄 😀 🙂 😐 ☹️ 😟 😠

I'm Looking Forward To the Day Because: ______________________

____

____

Three Things I'm Grateful for Today
1. ______________________
2. ______________________
3. ______________________

The Nice Things From Today

I Did for Someone	Someone Did for Me
______________________	______________________
______________________	______________________
______________________	______________________

Notes and Thoughts on the Day

____

____

____

____

____

Tonight My Mood Is:	😄 😀 🙂 😐 ☹️ 😟 😠

Date: ______________________

This Morning My Mood Is: 😄 😃 🙂 😐 ☹️ 😢 😠

I'm Looking Forward To the Day Because: ______________________

Three Things I'm Grateful for Today

1. ______________________
2. ______________________
3. ______________________

The Nice Things From Today

I Did for Someone

Someone Did for Me

Notes and Thoughts on the Day

Tonight My Mood Is: 😄 😃 🙂 😐 ☹️ 😢 😠

Date: ______________________

This Morning My Mood Is:

I'm Looking Forward To the Day Because: ______________________

Three Things I'm Grateful for Today

1. ______________________
2. ______________________
3. ______________________

The Nice Things From Today

I Did for Someone

Someone Did for Me

Notes and Thoughts on the Day

Tonight My Mood Is:

Date: ______

This Morning My Mood Is:

I'm Looking Forward To the Day Because: ______

Three Things I'm Grateful for Today

1. ______

2. ______

3. ______

The Nice Things From Today

I Did for Someone

Someone Did for Me

Notes and Thoughts on the Day

Tonight My Mood Is:

Date:

This Morning My Mood Is:

I'm Looking Forward To the Day Because:

Three Things I'm Grateful for Today

1.

2.

3.

The Nice Things From Today

I Did for Someone

Someone Did for Me

Notes and Thoughts on the Day

Tonight My Mood Is:

Date:

This Morning My Mood Is:

I'm Looking Forward To the Day Because:

Three Things I'm Grateful for Today

1.

2.

3.

The Nice Things From Today

I Did for Someone

Someone Did for Me

Notes and Thoughts on the Day

Tonight My Mood Is:

Date: ____________________

This Morning My Mood Is:

I'm Looking Forward To the Day Because: ____________________

Three Things I'm Grateful for Today

1. ____________________
2. ____________________
3. ____________________

The Nice Things From Today

I Did for Someone	Someone Did for Me

Notes and Thoughts on the Day

Tonight My Mood Is:

Date: ______________________

This Morning My Mood Is:	😄 😀 🙂 😐 ☹️ 😢 😠

I'm Looking Forward To the Day Because: ______________________

____

____

Three Things I'm Grateful for Today

1. ______________________
2. ______________________
3. ______________________

The Nice Things From Today

I Did for Someone	Someone Did for Me
______________________	______________________
______________________	______________________
______________________	______________________

Notes and Thoughts on the Day

____

____

____

____

____

Tonight My Mood Is:	😄 😀 🙂 😐 ☹️ 😢 😠

Date: ____________________

This Morning My Mood Is:

I'm Looking Forward To the Day Because: ____________________

Three Things I'm Grateful for Today

1. ____________________
2. ____________________
3. ____________________

The Nice Things From Today

I Did for Someone

Someone Did for Me

Notes and Thoughts on the Day

Tonight My Mood Is:

Date: ______________________

This Morning My Mood Is: ☐ ☐ ☐ ☐ ☐ ☐ ☐

I'm Looking Forward To the Day Because: ______________________

Three Things I'm Grateful for Today

1. ______________________
2. ______________________
3. ______________________

The Nice Things From Today

I Did for Someone	Someone Did for Me

Notes and Thoughts on the Day

Tonight My Mood Is: ☐ ☐ ☐ ☐ ☐ ☐ ☐

Date:

This Morning My Mood Is:

I'm Looking Forward To the Day Because:

Three Things I'm Grateful for Today

1.

2.

3.

The Nice Things From Today

I Did for Someone

Someone Did for Me

Notes and Thoughts on the Day

Tonight My Mood Is:

Date: ____________

This Morning My Mood Is:

I'm Looking Forward To the Day Because: ____________

Three Things I'm Grateful for Today

1. ____________

2. ____________

3. ____________

The Nice Things From Today

I Did for Someone

Someone Did for Me

Notes and Thoughts on the Day

Tonight My Mood Is:

Date:

This Morning My Mood Is:

I'm Looking Forward To the Day Because:

Three Things I'm Grateful for Today

1.

2.

3.

The Nice Things From Today

I Did for Someone

Someone Did for Me

Notes and Thoughts on the Day

Tonight My Mood Is:

Date: ______________________

This Morning My Mood Is:

I'm Looking Forward To the Day Because: ______________________

Three Things I'm Grateful for Today

1. ______________________

2. ______________________

3. ______________________

The Nice Things From Today

I Did for Someone

Someone Did for Me

Notes and Thoughts on the Day

Tonight My Mood Is:

Date:

This Morning My Mood Is:

I'm Looking Forward To the Day Because:

Three Things I'm Grateful for Today

1.
2.
3.

The Nice Things From Today

I Did for Someone

Someone Did for Me

Notes and Thoughts on the Day

Tonight My Mood Is:

Date: ____________________

This Morning My Mood Is:

I'm Looking Forward To the Day Because: ____________________

Three Things I'm Grateful for Today

1. ____________________
2. ____________________
3. ____________________

The Nice Things From Today

I Did for Someone

Someone Did for Me

Notes and Thoughts on the Day

Tonight My Mood Is:

Date: ____________________

This Morning My Mood Is: 😄 😃 🙂 😐 ☹️ 😢 😠

I'm Looking Forward To the Day Because: ____________________

Three Things I'm Grateful for Today

1. ____________________
2. ____________________
3. ____________________

The Nice Things From Today

I Did for Someone	Someone Did for Me

Notes and Thoughts on the Day

Tonight My Mood Is: 😄 😃 🙂 😐 ☹️ 😢 😠

Date: ______________________

This Morning My Mood Is:

I'm Looking Forward To the Day Because: ______________________

Three Things I'm Grateful for Today

1. ______________________
2. ______________________
3. ______________________

The Nice Things From Today

I Did for Someone

Someone Did for Me

Notes and Thoughts on the Day

Tonight My Mood Is:       

Date: ____________________

This Morning My Mood Is:

I'm Looking Forward To the Day Because: ____________________

Three Things I'm Grateful for Today

1. ____________________
2. ____________________
3. ____________________

The Nice Things From Today

I Did for Someone

Someone Did for Me

Notes and Thoughts on the Day

Tonight My Mood Is:

Date: ____________________

This Morning My Mood Is:

I'm Looking Forward To the Day Because: ____________________

Three Things I'm Grateful for Today

1. ____________________
2. ____________________
3. ____________________

The Nice Things From Today

I Did for Someone

Someone Did for Me

Notes and Thoughts on the Day

Tonight My Mood Is:

Date: ______________________

This Morning My Mood Is:

I'm Looking Forward To the Day Because: ______________________

Three Things I'm Grateful for Today

1. ______________________
2. ______________________
3. ______________________

The Nice Things From Today

I Did for Someone	Someone Did for Me

Notes and Thoughts on the Day

Tonight My Mood Is:

Date: ______________________

This Morning My Mood Is:

I'm Looking Forward To the Day Because: ______________________

Three Things I'm Grateful for Today

1. ______________________
2. ______________________
3. ______________________

The Nice Things From Today

I Did for Someone	Someone Did for Me

Notes and Thoughts on the Day

Tonight My Mood Is:

Date: ____________

This Morning My Mood Is:

I'm Looking Forward To the Day Because: ____________

Three Things I'm Grateful for Today

1. ____________
2. ____________
3. ____________

The Nice Things From Today

I Did for Someone	Someone Did for Me

Notes and Thoughts on the Day

Tonight My Mood Is:

Date: ____________________

This Morning My Mood Is:

I'm Looking Forward To the Day Because: ____________________

Three Things I'm Grateful for Today

1. ____________________
2. ____________________
3. ____________________

The Nice Things From Today

I Did for Someone

Someone Did for Me

Notes and Thoughts on the Day

Tonight My Mood Is:

Date:

This Morning My Mood Is:

I'm Looking Forward To the Day Because:

Three Things I'm Grateful for Today

1.

2.

3.

The Nice Things From Today

I Did for Someone

Someone Did for Me

Notes and Thoughts on the Day

Tonight My Mood Is:

Date: ______________________

This Morning My Mood Is: 😄 😀 🙂 😐 🙁 😢 😠

I'm Looking Forward To the Day Because: ______________________

____

____

Three Things I'm Grateful for Today

1. ______________________
2. ______________________
3. ______________________

The Nice Things From Today

I Did for Someone	Someone Did for Me

Notes and Thoughts on the Day

____

____

____

____

____

Tonight My Mood Is: 😄 😀 🙂 😐 🙁 😢 😠

Date:

This Morning My Mood Is:

I'm Looking Forward To the Day Because:

Three Things I'm Grateful for Today

1.

2.

3.

The Nice Things From Today

I Did for Someone

Someone Did for Me

Notes and Thoughts on the Day

Tonight My Mood Is:

Date: ______________________

This Morning My Mood Is:

I'm Looking Forward To the Day Because: ______________________

Three Things I'm Grateful for Today

1. ______________________
2. ______________________
3. ______________________

The Nice Things From Today

I Did for Someone	Someone Did for Me

Notes and Thoughts on the Day

Tonight My Mood Is:

Date: ____________________

This Morning My Mood Is:

I'm Looking Forward To the Day Because: ____________________

Three Things I'm Grateful for Today

1. ____________________

2. ____________________

3. ____________________

The Nice Things From Today

I Did for Someone

Someone Did for Me

Notes and Thoughts on the Day

Tonight My Mood Is:

Date: ____________

This Morning My Mood Is:

I'm Looking Forward To the Day Because: ____________

Three Things I'm Grateful for Today

1. ____________
2. ____________
3. ____________

The Nice Things From Today

I Did for Someone

Someone Did for Me

Notes and Thoughts on the Day

Tonight My Mood Is:

Date: ____________________

This Morning My Mood Is:

I'm Looking Forward To the Day Because: ____________________

Three Things I'm Grateful for Today

1. ____________________
2. ____________________
3. ____________________

The Nice Things From Today

I Did for Someone

Someone Did for Me

Notes and Thoughts on the Day

Tonight My Mood Is:

Date: ______________________

This Morning My Mood Is: 😄 😃 🙂 😐 ☹️ 😟 😠

I'm Looking Forward To the Day Because: ______________________

____

____

Three Things I'm Grateful for Today

1. ______________________

2. ______________________

3. ______________________

The Nice Things From Today

I Did for Someone

____

____

____

Someone Did for Me

____

____

____

Notes and Thoughts on the Day

____

____

____

____

____

Tonight My Mood Is: 😄 😃 🙂 😐 ☹️ 😟 😠

Date: ______________________

This Morning My Mood Is:

I'm Looking Forward To the Day Because: ______________________

Three Things I'm Grateful for Today

1. ______________________
2. ______________________
3. ______________________

The Nice Things From Today

I Did for Someone

Someone Did for Me

Notes and Thoughts on the Day

Tonight My Mood Is:

Date:

This Morning My Mood Is:

I'm Looking Forward To the Day Because:

Three Things I'm Grateful for Today

1.

2.

3.

The Nice Things From Today

I Did for Someone

Someone Did for Me

Notes and Thoughts on the Day

Tonight My Mood Is:

Date:

This Morning My Mood Is:

I'm Looking Forward To the Day Because:

Three Things I'm Grateful for Today

1.

2.

3.

The Nice Things From Today

I Did for Someone

Someone Did for Me

Notes and Thoughts on the Day

Tonight My Mood Is:

Date: ______________________

This Morning My Mood Is:

I'm Looking Forward To the Day Because: ______________________

Three Things I'm Grateful for Today

1. ______________________
2. ______________________
3. ______________________

The Nice Things From Today

I Did for Someone

Someone Did for Me

Notes and Thoughts on the Day

Tonight My Mood Is:       

Date: ____________________

This Morning My Mood Is:

I'm Looking Forward To the Day Because: ____________________

Three Things I'm Grateful for Today

1. ____________________
2. ____________________
3. ____________________

The Nice Things From Today

I Did for Someone

Someone Did for Me

Notes and Thoughts on the Day

Tonight My Mood Is:

Date: ____________________

This Morning My Mood Is:

I'm Looking Forward To the Day Because: ____________________

Three Things I'm Grateful for Today

1. ____________________
2. ____________________
3. ____________________

The Nice Things From Today

I Did for Someone

Someone Did for Me

Notes and Thoughts on the Day

Tonight My Mood Is:

Date: ____________________

This Morning My Mood Is:	😄 😀 🙂 😐 ☹️ 😟 😫

I'm Looking Forward To the Day Because: ____________________

____

____

Three Things I'm Grateful for Today
1. ____________________
2. ____________________
3. ____________________

The Nice Things From Today

I Did for Someone	Someone Did for Me
____________________	____________________
____________________	____________________
____________________	____________________

Notes and Thoughts on the Day

____

____

____

____

____

Tonight My Mood Is:	😄 😀 🙂 😐 ☹️ 😟 😫

Date:

This Morning My Mood Is:

I'm Looking Forward To the Day Because:

Three Things I'm Grateful for Today

1.
2.
3.

The Nice Things From Today

I Did for Someone

Someone Did for Me

Notes and Thoughts on the Day

Tonight My Mood Is:

Date: ____________________

This Morning My Mood Is:

I'm Looking Forward To the Day Because: ____________________

Three Things I'm Grateful for Today

1. ____________________
2. ____________________
3. ____________________

The Nice Things From Today

I Did for Someone

Someone Did for Me

Notes and Thoughts on the Day

Tonight My Mood Is:       

Date: ____________

This Morning My Mood Is:

I'm Looking Forward To the Day Because: ____________

Three Things I'm Grateful for Today

1. ____________
2. ____________
3. ____________

The Nice Things From Today

I Did for Someone

Someone Did for Me

Notes and Thoughts on the Day

Tonight My Mood Is:

Date: ______________________

This Morning My Mood Is: 😄 😀 🙂 😐 🙁 😵 😠

I'm Looking Forward To the Day Because: ______________________

____

____

Three Things I'm Grateful for Today

1. ______________________

2. ______________________

3. ______________________

The Nice Things From Today

I Did for Someone

____

____

____

Someone Did for Me

____

____

____

Notes and Thoughts on the Day

____

____

____

____

____

Tonight My Mood Is: 😄 😀 🙂 😐 🙁 😵 😠

Date: ____________________

This Morning My Mood Is:

I'm Looking Forward To the Day Because: ____________________

Three Things I'm Grateful for Today

1. ____________________
2. ____________________
3. ____________________

The Nice Things From Today

I Did for Someone

Someone Did for Me

Notes and Thoughts on the Day

Tonight My Mood Is:

Date: ____________________

This Morning My Mood Is:	😄 😀 🙂 😐 ☹️ 😵 😠

I'm Looking Forward To the Day Because: ____________________

____

____

Three Things I'm Grateful for Today

1. ____________________
2. ____________________
3. ____________________

The Nice Things From Today

I Did for Someone	Someone Did for Me
____________________	____________________
____________________	____________________
____________________	____________________

Notes and Thoughts on the Day

____

____

____

____

____

Tonight My Mood Is:	😄 😀 🙂 😐 ☹️ 😵 😠

Date: ____________________

This Morning My Mood Is:

I'm Looking Forward To the Day Because: ____________________

____

____

Three Things I'm Grateful for Today

1. ____________________
2. ____________________
3. ____________________

The Nice Things From Today

I Did for Someone

____

____

____

Someone Did for Me

____

____

____

Notes and Thoughts on the Day

____

____

____

____

____

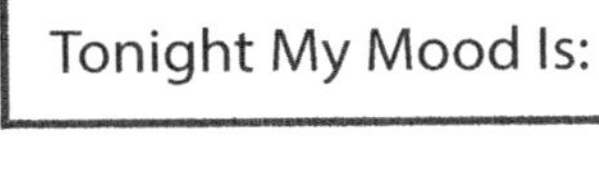

Tonight My Mood Is:

Date:

This Morning My Mood Is:

I'm Looking Forward To the Day Because:

Three Things I'm Grateful for Today

1.

2.

3.

The Nice Things From Today

I Did for Someone

Someone Did for Me

Notes and Thoughts on the Day

Tonight My Mood Is:

Date: ____________________

This Morning My Mood Is:

I'm Looking Forward To the Day Because: ____________________

Three Things I'm Grateful for Today

1. ____________________
2. ____________________
3. ____________________

The Nice Things From Today

I Did for Someone

Someone Did for Me

Notes and Thoughts on the Day

Tonight My Mood Is:

Date: ____________________

This Morning My Mood Is: ☐ ☐ ☐ ☐ ☐ ☐ ☐

I'm Looking Forward To the Day Because: ____________________

Three Things I'm Grateful for Today

1. ____________________
2. ____________________
3. ____________________

The Nice Things From Today

I Did for Someone	Someone Did for Me

Notes and Thoughts on the Day

Tonight My Mood Is: ☐ ☐ ☐ ☐ ☐ ☐ ☐

Date:

This Morning My Mood Is:

I'm Looking Forward To the Day Because:

Three Things I'm Grateful for Today

1.

2.

3.

The Nice Things From Today

I Did for Someone

Someone Did for Me

Notes and Thoughts on the Day

Tonight My Mood Is:

Date: ______________________

This Morning My Mood Is:

I'm Looking Forward To the Day Because: ______________________

Three Things I'm Grateful for Today

1. ______________________
2. ______________________
3. ______________________

The Nice Things From Today

I Did for Someone

Someone Did for Me

Notes and Thoughts on the Day

Tonight My Mood Is:

Date: ____________________

This Morning My Mood Is:

I'm Looking Forward To the Day Because: ____________________

Three Things I'm Grateful for Today

1. ____________________
2. ____________________
3. ____________________

The Nice Things From Today

I Did for Someone

Someone Did for Me

Notes and Thoughts on the Day

Tonight My Mood Is:

Date:

This Morning My Mood Is:

I'm Looking Forward To the Day Because:

Three Things I'm Grateful for Today

1.

2.

3.

The Nice Things From Today

I Did for Someone

Someone Did for Me

Notes and Thoughts on the Day

Tonight My Mood Is:

Date: ______________________

This Morning My Mood Is: ☐ ☐ ☐ ☐ ☐ ☐ ☐

I'm Looking Forward To the Day Because: ______________________

____

____

Three Things I'm Grateful for Today

1. ______________________

2. ______________________

3. ______________________

The Nice Things From Today

I Did for Someone

____

____

____

Someone Did for Me

____

____

____

Notes and Thoughts on the Day

____

____

____

____

____

Tonight My Mood Is: ☐ ☐ ☐ ☐ ☐ ☐ ☐

Date:

This Morning My Mood Is:

I'm Looking Forward To the Day Because:

Three Things I'm Grateful for Today

1.

2.

3.

The Nice Things From Today

I Did for Someone

Someone Did for Me

Notes and Thoughts on the Day

Tonight My Mood Is:

Date: ______________________

This Morning My Mood Is:

I'm Looking Forward To the Day Because: ______________________

Three Things I'm Grateful for Today

1. ______________________

2. ______________________

3. ______________________

The Nice Things From Today

I Did for Someone	Someone Did for Me

Notes and Thoughts on the Day

Tonight My Mood Is:

Date: ______________________

This Morning My Mood Is: 😄 😃 🙂 😐 🙁 😵 😠

I'm Looking Forward To the Day Because: ______________________

____

____

Three Things I'm Grateful for Today

1. ______________________

2. ______________________

3. ______________________

The Nice Things From Today

I Did for Someone

____

____

____

Someone Did for Me

____

____

____

Notes and Thoughts on the Day

____

____

____

____

____

Tonight My Mood Is: 😄 😃 🙂 😐 🙁 😵 😠

Date: ____________________

This Morning My Mood Is:

I'm Looking Forward To the Day Because: ____________________

Three Things I'm Grateful for Today

1. ____________________

2. ____________________

3. ____________________

The Nice Things From Today

I Did for Someone

Someone Did for Me

Notes and Thoughts on the Day

Tonight My Mood Is:

Date: ______________________

This Morning My Mood Is:

I'm Looking Forward To the Day Because: ______________________

Three Things I'm Grateful for Today

1. ______________________

2. ______________________

3. ______________________

The Nice Things From Today

I Did for Someone

Someone Did for Me

Notes and Thoughts on the Day

Tonight My Mood Is:      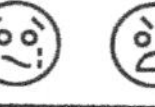

Date: ______________________

This Morning My Mood Is:

I'm Looking Forward To the Day Because: ______________________

Three Things I'm Grateful for Today

1. ______________________
2. ______________________
3. ______________________

The Nice Things From Today

I Did for Someone

Someone Did for Me

Notes and Thoughts on the Day

Tonight My Mood Is:

Date: ______________________

This Morning My Mood Is:

I'm Looking Forward To the Day Because: ______________________

Three Things I'm Grateful for Today

1. ______________________
2. ______________________
3. ______________________

The Nice Things From Today

I Did for Someone

Someone Did for Me

Notes and Thoughts on the Day

Tonight My Mood Is:

Date: ____________________

This Morning My Mood Is:

I'm Looking Forward To the Day Because: ____________________

Three Things I'm Grateful for Today

1. ____________________

2. ____________________

3. ____________________

The Nice Things From Today

I Did for Someone

Someone Did for Me

Notes and Thoughts on the Day

Tonight My Mood Is:

Date: ______________________

This Morning My Mood Is:

I'm Looking Forward To the Day Because: ______________________

Three Things I'm Grateful for Today

1. ______________________

2. ______________________

3. ______________________

The Nice Things From Today

I Did for Someone

Someone Did for Me

Notes and Thoughts on the Day

Tonight My Mood Is:

Date:

This Morning My Mood Is:

I'm Looking Forward To the Day Because:

Three Things I'm Grateful for Today

1.

2.

3.

The Nice Things From Today

I Did for Someone

Someone Did for Me

Notes and Thoughts on the Day

Tonight My Mood Is:

Date: ____________________

This Morning My Mood Is:

I'm Looking Forward To the Day Because: ____________________

Three Things I'm Grateful for Today

1. ____________________
2. ____________________
3. ____________________

The Nice Things From Today

I Did for Someone

Someone Did for Me

Notes and Thoughts on the Day

Tonight My Mood Is:       

Date: ____________________

This Morning My Mood Is:

I'm Looking Forward To the Day Because: ____________________

Three Things I'm Grateful for Today

1. ____________________

2. ____________________

3. ____________________

The Nice Things From Today

I Did for Someone

Someone Did for Me

Notes and Thoughts on the Day

Tonight My Mood Is:

Date: ____________________

This Morning My Mood Is:

I'm Looking Forward To the Day Because: ____________________

Three Things I'm Grateful for Today

1. ____________________
2. ____________________
3. ____________________

The Nice Things From Today

I Did for Someone

Someone Did for Me

Notes and Thoughts on the Day

Tonight My Mood Is:       

Date: ______________________

This Morning My Mood Is:

I'm Looking Forward To the Day Because: ______________________

____

____

Three Things I'm Grateful for Today

1. ______________________
2. ______________________
3. ______________________

The Nice Things From Today

I Did for Someone	Someone Did for Me

Notes and Thoughts on the Day

____

____

____

____

____

Tonight My Mood Is:

Date: ____________________

This Morning My Mood Is:

I'm Looking Forward To the Day Because: ____________________

Three Things I'm Grateful for Today

1. ____________________
2. ____________________
3. ____________________

The Nice Things From Today

I Did for Someone

Someone Did for Me

Notes and Thoughts on the Day

Tonight My Mood Is:       

Date: ______________________

This Morning My Mood Is:

I'm Looking Forward To the Day Because: ______________________

Three Things I'm Grateful for Today

1. ______________________
2. ______________________
3. ______________________

The Nice Things From Today

I Did for Someone	Someone Did for Me

Notes and Thoughts on the Day

Tonight My Mood Is:

Date: ____________________

This Morning My Mood Is:

I'm Looking Forward To the Day Because: ____________________

Three Things I'm Grateful for Today

1. ____________________
2. ____________________
3. ____________________

The Nice Things From Today

I Did for Someone

Someone Did for Me

Notes and Thoughts on the Day

Tonight My Mood Is:

Date: ______________________

This Morning My Mood Is:

I'm Looking Forward To the Day Because: ______________________

Three Things I'm Grateful for Today

1. ______________________

2. ______________________

3. ______________________

The Nice Things From Today

I Did for Someone

Someone Did for Me

Notes and Thoughts on the Day

Tonight My Mood Is:

Date: ____________________

This Morning My Mood Is:

I'm Looking Forward To the Day Because: ____________________

Three Things I'm Grateful for Today

1. ____________________

2. ____________________

3. ____________________

The Nice Things From Today

I Did for Someone

Someone Did for Me

Notes and Thoughts on the Day

Tonight My Mood Is:

Date: ______________________

This Morning My Mood Is:

I'm Looking Forward To the Day Because: ______________________

Three Things I'm Grateful for Today

1. ______________________
2. ______________________
3. ______________________

The Nice Things From Today

I Did for Someone

Someone Did for Me

Notes and Thoughts on the Day

Tonight My Mood Is:       

Date:

This Morning My Mood Is:

I'm Looking Forward To the Day Because:

Three Things I'm Grateful for Today

1.
2.
3.

The Nice Things From Today

I Did for Someone

Someone Did for Me

Notes and Thoughts on the Day

Tonight My Mood Is: